W9-BPQ-877

Festivals of the *World*

CHILE

Gareth Stevens Publishing
MILWAUKEE

Written by
SUSAN RORAFF

Edited by
AUDREY LIM

Designed by
HASNAH MOHD ESA

Picture research by
SUSAN JANE MANUEL

First published in North America in 1998 by
Gareth Stevens Publishing
1555 North RiverCenter Drive, Suite 201
Milwaukee, Wisconsin 53212 USA

For a free color catalog describing Gareth
Stevens' list of high-quality books and multimedia
programs, call
1-800-542-2595 (USA)
or 1-800-461-9120 (Canada).
Gareth Stevens Publishing's Fax: (414) 225-0377.
See our catalog, too, on the World Wide Web:
http://gsinc.com

All rights reserved. No part of this book may be
reproduced or utilized in any form or by any
means electronic or mechanical, including
photocopying, recording, or by an information
storage and retrieval system, without permission
from the copyright owner.

© TIMES EDITIONS PTE LTD 1998
Originated and designed by
Times Books International
an imprint of Times Editions Pte Ltd
Times Centre, 1 New Industrial Road
Singapore 536196
Printed in Singapore

Library of Congress Cataloging-in-Publication Data:
Roraff, Susan.
Chile / by Susan Roraff.
p. cm.—(Festivals of the world)
Includes bibliographical references and index.
Summary: Describes how the culture of Chile is
reflected in its many festivals, including Tangata
Manu, Fiestas Patrias, and La Tirana.
ISBN 0-8368-2012-6 (lib. bdg.)
1. Festivals—Chile—Juvenile literature. 2. Chile—
Social life and customs—Juvenile literature. [1.
Festivals—Chile. 2. Holidays—Chile. 3. Chile—
Social life and customs.] I. Title. II. Series.
GT4834.A2R67 1998
394.26983—dc21 98-5299

1 2 3 4 5 6 7 8 9 02 01 00 99 98

CONTENTS

It's Festival Time . . .

The Spanish word for festival or party is *fiesta* [fee-ESS-tah], and Chileans enjoy such celebrations all year round. Some are religious celebrations that bring families together, while others give Chileans a chance to display national pride. Different regions of Chile celebrate different fiestas. Let's join the Chileans and see how the music, colors, and magic of their festivals fill their long and narrow country.

WHERE'S CHILE?

C hile is located in South America. It is bordered by the Pacific Ocean to the west, and the Andes mountain range to the east. Easter Island, the Juan Fernández Archipelago, and a section of **Antarctica** are also part of Chile.

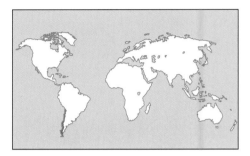

Who are the Chileans?

When Spanish explorers arrived in the 16th century, there were many different native peoples living in what is now Chile. Chile was a **colony** of Spain for over 200 years. Many of the **indigenous** peoples died from diseases the Spanish brought. Some indigenous groups have even completely disappeared. The country gained its independence in 1818. Today, the Mapuche [mah-POO-chay] is the largest native group in Chile. Most Chileans have both native Indian and Spanish ancestry. Other immigrants to Chile came from Great Britain, Italy, France, and Palestine. There is also a large German community living in the south, which still speaks German and follows German **customs**.

These two Chilean girls are fussing over their cat.

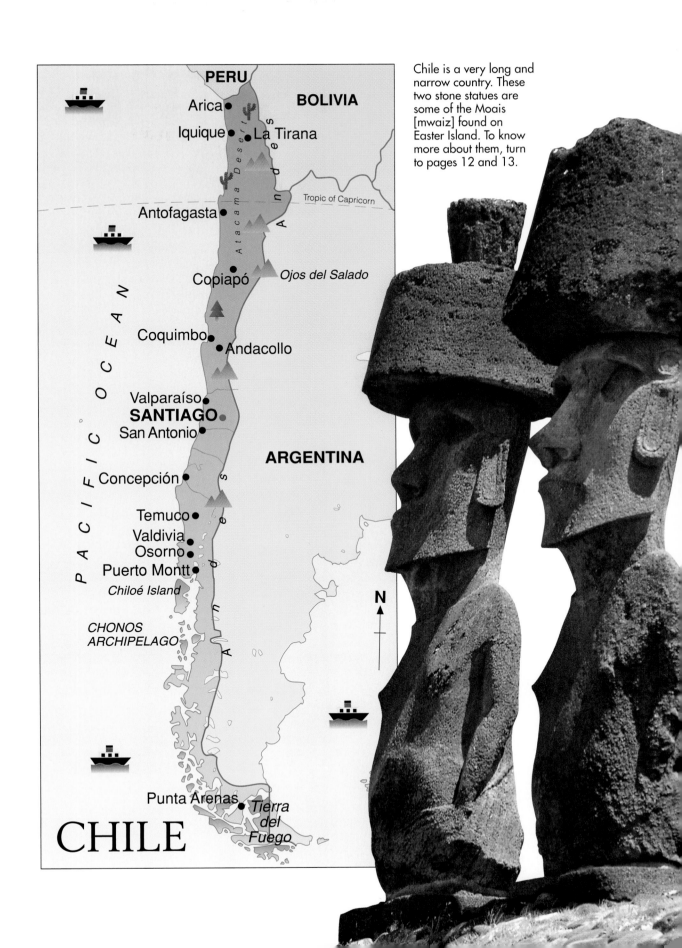

Chile is a very long and narrow country. These two stone statues are some of the Moais [mwaiz] found on Easter Island. To know more about them, turn to pages 12 and 13.

PERU

BOLIVIA

Arica

Iquique

La Tirana

Atacama Desert

Tropic of Capricorn

Antofagasta

Andes

Copiapó

Ojos del Salado

Coquimbo

Andacollo

Valparaíso

SANTIAGO

San Antonio

ARGENTINA

Concepción

Andes

Temuco

Valdivia

Osorno

Puerto Montt

Chiloé Island

PACIFIC OCEAN

CHONOS ARCHIPELAGO

Andes

N

Punta Arenas

Tierra del Fuego

CHILE

WHEN'S THE FIESTA?

WINTER

✪ **FEAST OF SAINT PETER**—In many small villages along the Pacific Ocean, fishing boats are decorated and an image of Saint Peter, the patron saint of fishermen, is carried around the bay, in the hope that the fish catch will be **bountiful**.

✪ **LA TIRANA**—This festival takes place in the desert where the weather is always like spring, even in winter.

Hey, my friend, what's going on?

Don't look back, but I think a festival's headed our way!

SPRING

✪ **TANGATA MANU**—The inhabitants of Easter Island, located in the Pacific Ocean, celebrated this festival annually, also known as the Birdman festival.

✪ **FIESTAS PATRIAS**—This festival is made up of both National Day and Army day. There are exciting rodeos and parades to watch on these two days.

✪ **COLUMBUS DAY**—Celebrates Christopher Columbus' arrival in the Americas.

SUMMER

- ✪ **ALL SOULS DAY**—Many Chileans visit cemeteries to pay their respects to loved ones who have died.
- ✪ **IMMACULATE CONCEPTION**—Many people from Santiago walk 45 miles (72.5 kilometers) to the Lo Vásquez Shrine to thank the Virgin Mary for answering their prayers.
- ✪ **CHRISTMAS**—Many Chilean families attend midnight mass on Christmas Eve and open presents after that. Since it is the middle of summer, many families either have barbecues or spend Christmas day at the beach.
- ✪ **NEW YEAR'S EVE**—At midnight, fireworks explode all over Chile. For good luck in the coming year, many Chileans eat a spoonful of lentils. Other Chileans put money in their pockets hoping to be rich in the new year. At midnight, Chileans celebrate with close family members. After that, they visit extended family members and friends until the wee hours of the morning.
- ✪ **FESTIVAL DE LA CANCIÓN**—The largest musical contest in Latin America, with participants from all over the world. The winner gets the "Seagull Trophy."

What do you think of my colorful costume?

AUTUMN

- ✪ **NGILLATUN**
- ✪ **CARNIVAL**—Only celebrated in northern Chile and heavily influenced by the Aymara Indians, Carnival is the last big party before the 40 days of Lent begin.
- ✪ **EASTER AND CUASIMODO**
- ✪ **NAVY DAY**—On this day, Chile honors its most famous naval hero, Arturo Prat. Even though he was outmatched during a battle in the War of the Pacific in 1879, he refused to surrender.

LA TIRANA

For three days every July, the small village of La Tirana [lah tee-RAH-nah] in northern Chile welcomes over 70,000 people in celebration of the festival La Tirana. Many different dance groups, called *chinos* [CHEE-nohs], parade through the village. This parade ends at the shrine **dedicated** to the Virgen del Carmen of La Tirana.

The tyrant

La Tirana means "the **tyrant**." The town is named after an Indian princess who fell in love with a Spanish miner and converted to Catholicism. She became a tyrant, forcing her subjects to also become Catholic. Later, she and the miner were killed. Before this, she begged they be buried together near the creek where she had been baptized. A cross marked this spot and years later, a priest, upon hearing the legend, built a temple in honor of the princess and the Virgen del Carmen.

The chinos wear fantastic costumes and masks. They dance to honor the Virgin Mary and to keep a promise they made to Her.

The chinos

Dance and musical groups called chinos are societies or brotherhoods that are guardians of the Virgin Mary. The dancers wear elaborate, colorful, and exotic costumes. Some of these costumes are similar to clothing worn by conquistadors, American Indians, Chinese, or even ancient Romans. The costumes are made of silk and decorated with **dazzling** jewels and flowing capes. One of the best is the devil costume that has a fearsome devil mask with great bulging eyes. Each dancer acts like a character in a specific story. The tale is told through dancing and is usually about colonial or religious conflict. The dancers dance for three days, stopping only to change costumes or eat. They believe their faith gives them energy to dance continuously.

Musicians encourage the dancers with loud, repetitious music. They play trumpets, trombones, *bombos* [BOM-bohs] or large drums, *quenas* [KAY-nahs] or flutes, *zampoñas* [sahm-POH-nyas] or panflutes, cymbals, triangles, and whistles. People pray, sing, and chant along with the music.

The chinos practice hard all year round to give a polished performance. The dancers often decorate their costumes with roses, pompoms, and tassels.

Honoring a promise

The chinos begin dancing at the entrance of the village and slowly make their way to the door of the shrine dedicated to the Virgen del Carmen. All who participate do so to honor the Virgin Mary and to thank her for answering their prayers.

The Virgin Mary is very important to many Chileans. It is believed that she often helps those who pray to Her because she is the Holy Mother, and is very loving and caring. Many promise to perform some act of **sacrifice** in her name if a prayer is answered or if a favor is granted. Those who dance during the festival of La Tirana do so to fulfill such a promise.

Above: There are other festivals in Chile that honor the Virgin Mary. An example is the Festival of Andacollo.

Right: The chinos can be differentiated by their costumes. Each group has about 15 to 50 dancers.

A mixture of cultures

The La Tirana festival is a blend of Andean and Spanish cultures. It is based primarily on native beliefs and customs. Many of the musical instruments, costumes, and dances that are part of this festival are derived from the people of the Andes mountains.

When Jesuit priests converted the native people to Catholicism, they allowed the natives to continue celebrating their traditional dances. However, these Andean dances were combined with Spanish dances mainly from the region of Andalusia and the priests gave the dances a very Christian meaning. These new dances then became an offering to the Virgin Mary.

The masks worn by the chinos are made of papier-mâché and take a long time to make.

Think about this
The Indians in northern Chile, Bolivia, and southern Peru share many of the same musical instruments. One such instrument is the *charango* (cha-RAHN-go). This is a small stringed instrument made from an armadillo. Do you know what an armadillo looks like?

TANGATA MANU

Easter Island is located in the middle of the Pacific Ocean. The people who once lived there celebrated the Tangata Manu [tahn-GAH-tah MAH-noo] or Birdman festival. They believed Tangata Manu was a representative of the god, Makemake [MAH-kay-MAH-kay].

Below: An inhabitant of Easter Island with ceremonial paintings on his body.

Right: Petroglyphs are large drawings carved on rocks. This is a carving of a turtle.

Find that egg

In the past, an annual contest was held between the island's different clans. One member of each tribe swam to a nearby island to search for the first egg laid by the Manu Tara [mah-new TAH-rah], a sacred bird. It usually took about a month before one of the searchers actually found the egg. The winner was the first to swim back to shore with the egg strapped to his forehead to present to his chief. The chief was then named "Birdman" for the year and was believed to be especially blessed by Makemake. The Birdman ritual is no longer performed annually because it is very dangerous. Today, only parts of the ceremony are re-enacted once in a while.

The Moais

The first settlers on the island were Polynesians. In A.D. 400, they sailed across the Pacific Ocean in canoes made from **bark**. They called themselves Rapa Nui [RAH-pah NEW-ee] and called their new home Te Pito O Te Henua [tay PEE-toh oh tay HEN-ew-ah], which means "Bellybutton of the World" in Polynesian. The island is famous for the very large Moais that were already knocked down when found. Moais are very tall stone carvings of mostly male heads and torsos with hats. They are images of dead chiefs or gods. There are also many carvings of the Birdman found all over the island. The Birdman has a man's body, a bird's head, and holds an egg in its hand.

Right: Feather headdresses are an important part of traditional Rapa Nui costumes.

13

Above: A girl displays some corals, shells, and other handicrafts to two tourists. Can you see the miniature Moais she has by the side?

Language and clothing

The Rapa Nui had a written language similar to the hieroglyphs used by the ancient Egyptians. Pictures were carved onto wooden tablets as a way of telling stories. In the past, the people of Easter Island wore very little clothing. They decorated their bodies with many tattoos. Faces, necks, chests, stomachs, backs, and legs were covered with geometrical designs or pictures of birds or people. They also used feathers and shells as headdresses and jewelry.

Left: As in other parts of Polynesia, tropical flowers add to the beauty of the wearer.

Ecological disaster

Easter Island is very far away from any other land. The people who once lived there depended on the island for everything because they did not trade with anyone else. The islanders cultivated farms for food and built their own houses. They cut down many trees to build houses and canoes, as well as fires to cook their food. They also used tree trunks to roll the large Moais across the island. As the population grew, the amount of food was not enough to feed everyone. When all the trees were gone, they could not build canoes to leave the island. Some people believe war broke out between the clans, and they were forced into **cannibalism**. Many think this happened when the large Moais were pushed over and the Birdman cult began.

Think about this
Easter Island got its name from the fact that the first European to arrive here, a Dutchman, landed on Easter Sunday. Fifty years later, the Spanish arrived to take many of the Rapa Nui as slaves to Peru. Many more died from diseases brought by the Spaniards. In 1877, only 111 people still lived on the island.

Below: An example of Polynesian art. This carving must have taken a long time to complete!

FIESTAS PATRIAS

N ational Day and Army Day, known together as Fiestas Patrias [fee-ESS-tahs pah-TREE-ahs], is the most important holiday in Chile. On September 18th, 1810, the first local government was formed while Chile was still a Spanish colony. Although it ruled in the name of the Spanish king who had been overthrown by the French, self-rule was an important step toward independence. In 1818, Chilean troops finally defeated the Spanish.

Fondas

Fondas [FOHN-dahs] are fairs set up all over Chile for a few weeks before National Day. There are many booths that sell food, drinks, souvenirs, and offer carnival-style games. In the center of the fair, there is a stage for a band and a big dance floor. Chileans eat, drink, and dance all night long.

Above: The large spurs of a huaso's boots.

Left: The *Cueca* [KWAY-kah] is the national dance of Chile and is danced continuously during Fiestas Patrias. It is a dance of courtship and is always danced to the music of the guitar, harp, and tambourine.

Huasos and rodeos

Huasos [WAH-sos], or cowboys, are one of the symbols of Chile. Most huasos live in the central part of the country where the land is good for raising cattle. Huasos wear very special clothing that is similar to the traditional dress worn in Andalusia in Spain. Huasos wear ponchos called *mantas* [MAN-tahs] over their black **pinstriped** pants, white shirts, and black jackets. They also wear large spurs on their boots. In summer, they wear straw hats and in winter, black felt hats.

To celebrate Fiestas Patrias, many huasos compete in rodeos. Chilean rodeo is very different from American rodeo. In Chile, the huaso earns points by pinning a calf against the wall of the arena with his horse. The number of points scored depends on the part of the horse touching the calf. For example, it is best if the rear of the horse pins the calf. No points are given if the horse uses its head.

Huasos hold their rodeos in a stadium or *medialuna* [MAY-dee-ah-LOO-nah]. This means "half moon" and is in reference to the stadium's shape.

Above: The Chilean army on parade.

Think about this

The Chilean flag has one white stripe, one red stripe, and a white star in the middle of a blue square in the upper left hand corner. These three colors are the traditional colors of a republic form of government. This means the country is ruled by the people and not by a king or queen. Can you name other countries with flags that also use the colors red, white, and blue?

Army Day

Army Day is celebrated on September 19th. In the largest park in Santiago, there is a big military parade where all the military schools, military regiments, tanks, jets, and cannons are put on display. The president officially presides over the parade. The army, navy, air force, and national police force all take part in the parade.

Springtime

September is a very festive month because of Fiestas Patrias, and also because it is the beginning of spring. Spring brings warm breezes, and Chilean flags are everywhere. There are many kite-flying contests. Kite strings are coated with crushed glass, and the goal is to cut your opponent's kite loose. Many children gather around the competitors to chase after kites as they fall to the ground.

Opposite: A more experienced huaso is teaching a younger huaso the art of riding a horse.

Below: Many typical Chilean foods are eaten during this time of the year. *Empanadas* [em-pah-NAH-dahs], meat- or cheese-filled turnovers, are an example.

EASTER

Easter is the holiest time of the year for Chileans, most of whom are Catholic. The week before Easter is called Semana Santa [say-MAH-nah SAN-ta] meaning Holy Week. This is when Catholics remember Jesus' death and resurrection. Families quietly celebrate Easter Sunday together. In small towns in central Chile, everyone pours out into the streets to celebrate Cuasimodo [kwah-zee-MOH-doh] the first Sunday following Easter Sunday.

Semana Santa

During Holy Week, many Chileans go to church to pray. To celebrate Semana Santa, children pull big dolls, representing Judas, in small carts and wagons around their neighborhood. They visit houses and ask for coins that **symbolize** the money Judas received in return for **betraying** Jesus to the Romans. The children get to keep the coins. At the end of the day, parents help their children burn the dolls.

Above: A shop's Easter display.

Left: During the Cuasimodo procession, children ride bicycles that are colorfully decorated.

20

Easter Sunday

On Easter Sunday, children from German families awake to find baskets filled with chocolates. They also take part in an Easter egg hunt. Children look for hidden eggs. These eggs are a sign of fertility. Today, more and more children who are not from German families also celebrate Easter this way.

Above: A cathedral in Santiago. Families go to mass on Easter Sunday to celebrate the resurrection of Jesus from the dead.

Cuasimodo

Cuasimodo is celebrated on the first Sunday following Easter Sunday. In many small towns and rural areas throughout central and southern Chile, the local priest leads a procession and gives Communion to those people who are too sick or too old to go to church. The priest rides in a carriage, and is surrounded by many huasos riding horses and carrying religious images. As a sign of respect, the huasos do not wear hats as they usually do. Instead, they tie scarves around their heads. The whole town takes part in the procession.

Left: A Cuasimodo procession in Santiago.

Think about this
To prepare themselves for Easter, Catholics celebrate Lent. Lent is a time of personal sacrifice and prayer that lasts for 40 days. Catholics are not allowed to eat meat on Fridays during Lent.

The days of bandits

Cuasimodo started over 100 years ago. Often, the priests visited people who could not go to church. They lived out in the country, far away from the town and other neighbors. During this time, many bandits roamed the land, stealing from farmers and priests. Several huasos would ride with the priest into the countryside to protect him from these thieves.

Today, there are no more bandits but Cuasimodo still allows the huasos to show off their horse-riding skills. After the procession through the village, many horse-riding contests are held.

Opposite: Huasos displaying their riding skills at a contest.

Below: A priest with outstretched arms, offering the sacrament during Cuasimodo.

NGILLATUN

T he Mapuche, meaning "people of the land," were the first people to live in central Chile. During autumn, when it is time to harvest the crops, the Mapuche perform a prayer ceremony called Ngillatun [gee-ya-TOON]. They pray to the spirit Pillán [pee-YAN], who is made up of all the spirits of the ancestors.

A *machi* [MAH-chee], a female priest, leads the ceremony. The whole town participates in the Ngillatun, and everyone paints their face blue and white. To the Mapuche, these colors have a special religious meaning. During the ceremony, there is music, singing, and dancing. In the past, an animal was sacrificed to please the spirit, but this custom no longer takes place. After the ceremony, there is a large party for everyone with lots of food and drinks.

Above and left: Mapuche women wear brightly colored clothing and have beautiful silver jewelry.

Opposite: Weaving a traditional Mapuche design on a vertical loom.

24

THINGS FOR YOU TO DO

Music plays an important role in almost all Chilean festivals. Would you like to create some music, too? Choose either the melodic sounds of the Andean zampoña or the monotone sound of the Mapuche *trutruka* [troo-TROO-kah]!

Traditional Andean musical instruments

The zampoña, the quena, the bombo, and the charango are used by the Aymara Indians who live in the mountains of northern Chile and other musicians. These instruments give their music a distinctive sound.

You too can create music by making your own zampoña! A zampoña is usually made with bamboo, but if that is too hard to find, you can use pieces of plastic hose or garden tubes. Depending on how big you want to make the zampoña, have an adult help you cut between four to eight pieces of tubing, each piece about an inch (2.5 centimeters) longer than the previous one. Plug the bottom of each tube with modeling clay, cork, or plasticine. Assemble the pieces in descending order of length, using either masking tape, or by tying them together with string or yarn. To play the instrument, blow across the top of the tubes—not into them. Move the zampoña back and forth to hear the different notes and invent your own song.

Musical instruments of the Mapuche

The Mapuche Indians created musical instruments for their rituals. One such instrument is the trutruka, a long trumpet, which is played during harvest festivals. The sound produced by the trutruka is believed to have mystical powers, and those who play it are called *Tuntaman* [tune-TAH-mahn].

The Mapuche make the trutruka out of long pieces of bamboo and the horn of a bull, but you can use a long hose or a plastic pipe, and a plastic bottle. The hose should be almost as tall as you are. Cut the bottom off the plastic bottle and slide the bottleneck over the end of the tube. Using masking tape, attach the bottle to the tube. The bottle should lie on the floor while you blow into the other end of the tube. Blow hard to hear the very deep, loud sound made by the Mapuche trutruka!

Things to look for in your library:

Andes Mountains (Wonders of the World). Rose Blue and Corinne Naden (Raintree/Steck-Vaughn, 1994).

Chile. Christopher Dwyer (Chelsea House Publishers, 1989).

Chile: Land of Poets and Patriots (Discovering Our Heritage). Irene Flum Galvin (Dillon Press, 1990).

Chile: Where the Land Ends. Marianne Pickering (Benchmark Books, 1997).

Land of the Llamas. (video).

Leyenda. Inti-Illimani (CBS Records).

Silent Sentinels: The Mystery of Easter Island. (video).

MAKE AN ARPILLERA

Many Chileans make *arpilleras* [ar-pee-YARE-ahs] to tell a story. Most are made out of scraps of old material sewn together, but you can make your own using glue and pieces of multi-colored felt. The picture on your right shows an arpillera. Use it as a guide to show Chileans having fun at Fiestas Patrias, or use your imagination and tell your own story.

You will need:
1. Pieces of different colored felt 10" x 12" (25 x 30 cm)
2. Glue
3. Scissors
4. Wax pencil

1

3

4

2

1 Using your wax pencil, draw the different shapes you want to have on your arpillera; for example, shapes of people and scenery. Then, cut them out with the scissors.

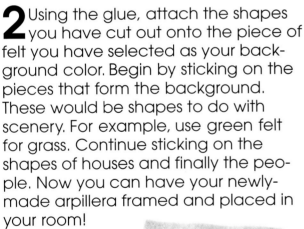

2 Using the glue, attach the shapes you have cut out onto the piece of felt you have selected as your background color. Begin by sticking on the pieces that form the background. These would be shapes to do with scenery. For example, use green felt for grass. Continue sticking on the shapes of houses and finally the people. Now you can have your newly-made arpillera framed and placed in your room!

MAKE LECHE CON PLÁTANO

Beginning with Fiestas Patrias and continuing all through summer, Chileans enjoy a drink called leche con plátano. This means milk with bananas. Celebrate your summer fiestas by whipping up a batch of leche con plátano to help cool you down!

You will need:
1. 1 cup (240 ml) very cold milk
2. 1 tablespoon sugar
3. 1 small banana
4. Measuring spoons
5. Measuring cup
6. Blender
7. Plate

6

1 & 5

2

4

3 & 7

1 Peel the banana and break it into small pieces.

2 Pour the milk into the blender. Add in the sugar as well.

3 Put the pieces of banana into the blender. Seal the top of the blender. Blend on LOW for a few seconds. The drink should be thick with some small chunks of banana. Pour into a glass and drink immediately. The drink must be very cold to cool you down during the long, hot summer!

GLOSSARY

Antarctica, 4	Continent engulfing the South Pole.
bark, 13	Outer layer of a tree trunk.
betraying, 20	Being disloyal to a friend and handing that person over to the enemy.
bountiful, 6	Plentiful and in abundance.
cannibalism, 15	When humans consume the flesh of other humans.
colony, 4	A territory subject to the power of another, more powerful, territory.
customs, 4	Traditions or practices.
dazzling, 9	Captivating, bewitching, and impressive.
dedicated, 8	Done in memory of.
indigenous, 4	Native.
pinstriped, 17	A design where long, thin lines run parallel along the fabric.
sacrifice, 10	Giving up something that is important to oneself.
symbolize, 20	To represent.
tyrant, 8	One who wields power unjustly or oppressively.

INDEX

Picture credits
A.N.A. Press Agency: 21; Camera Press: 1, 12 (top), 15, 16 (both), 17, 19 (both); Dave G. Houser: 2; Hutchison Library: 20 (bottom), 24 (bottom); Internationales Bildarchiv/Horst Von Irmer: 12 (bottom), 13 (both), 14 (both), 25; Life File: 4; Colleen Purcell: 3 (bottom), 6, 7 (both), 10 (bottom), 11, 18; South American Pictures: 20 (top), 22, 23 (both), 27; Tan Chung Lee: 5; Topham Picture Point: 24 (top); Mario Vergara: 3 (top), 8, 9, 10 (top)